Cattail Skyline

Also by Joanne Epp

Eigenheim

CATTAIL SKYLINE

Joanne Epp

TURNSTONE PRESS

Cattail Skyline

Turnstone Press
Artspace Building
206-100 Arthur Street
Winnipeg, MB
R3B 1H3 Canada
www.TurnstonePress.com

Turnstone Press gratefully acknowledges the assistance of the Canada Council for the Arts, the Manitoba Arts Council, the Government of Canada through the Canada Book Fund, and the Province of Manitoba through the Book Publishing Tax Credit and the Book Publisher Marketing Assistance Program.

Cover design: Melissa McIvor

Printed and bound in Canada.

Library and Archives Canada Cataloguing in Publication

Title: Cattail skyline / Joanne Epp.
Names: Epp, Joanne, 1963- author.
Description: Poems.
Identifiers: Canadiana (print) 20200410008 | Canadiana (ebook) 20200410024 | ISBN 9780888017239 (softcover) | ISBN 9780888017246 (EPUB) | ISBN 9780888017253 (Kindle) | ISBN 9780888017260 (PDF)
Classification: LCC PS8609.P65 C38 2021 | DDC C811/.6—dc23

MANITOBA ARTS COUNCIL
CONSEIL DES ARTS DU MANITOBA

Canada Council for the Arts | Conseil des arts du Canada

Funded by the Government of Canada
Financé par le gouvernement du Canada
Canada

Manitoba

MIX
Paper from responsible sources
FSC www.fsc.org FSC® C103567

For Gilbert Epp (1935–2020)

Contents

Settling into motion

Resisting the return to shore

Cattail Skyline

~ Cemetery road 1 ~

A crow call. Open space and a road. Not just any road, but this one leaving the little town where you went to high school, where you still come every summer. The road that passes a cluster of houses, an abandoned barn, harvested fields dotted with straw bales. This is the scene that appears when you hear, distant, a crow: the straight line stretching north; the ditches, noisy with frogs; the bush where deer hide until dusk. Up ahead, within a square enclosure of hedge, the cemetery. It's a clear day. Hot. Gravel crunches underfoot. Now and then a pickup passes, trailing dust. You sidestep to the edge, as far as you can without slipping into the ditch. The truck also moves aside. If your eyes meet the driver's you might wave. But mostly you're alone. Far back from the road, a clump of maple or green ash. A crow erupts from the branches. A scrap of black thrown against the sky.

How far can we follow

Hague Ferry

The ferry's a hidden thing, only half believed in
until the road dives into the sudden valley.
Density of dogwood and chokecherry
to right and left, and a warning: TEST BRAKES.
We've left the upper world, gone down
to where the sky has borders.

A sheet-metal raft, four cars square.
An engine to propel, a cable to guide
below the ceiling of canola fields.
The ferryman's silent, hardly seen:
the gesture of a single chain;
a signal to bring us on.

Lanigan Creek

Swaying on cattails, the blackbirds—
yellow-headed, red-winged—see it all:
their domain and one intruder.
I sidestep down the bank, crouch low.
Blackbirds whistle. I wait.

Flickers of movement. Footprints
dimple the surface of the stream.
Bubbles rise from mud; slivers of light
pierce green water. Mottled brown
shifts on brown. Red and blue
needles stitch the air. Coiled spires
of shells glide flat-footed,
infinitely slow.

Below the cattail skyline, time
becomes elastic. The silence hums.

Grass tickles my back. I am
invisible as a mountain.

Fort Carlton

Everyone knows it's a buffalo rubbing stone,
that boulder on top of the hill.
This is where the bison came
to scratch their behinds, massage
their woolly shoulders. Not rough like a tree,
but stronger. They could lean hard,
rub the itches out. *See this,*
says one of the boys, *the ground's*
hollowed out all around it. That's from their hoofs.
You mean hooves, a girl corrects him.

We know about glaciers from school.
We know they left rocks in odd places. *Erratics*,
the book called them. Eccentrics.
Strangers amid the grass and willows.

This one's chest-high on us, rubbed smooth
by generations of bison. We hoist ourselves up,
feel its warmth beneath us. We pick at
the lichen clinging to it, savouring
these few things we know.

Saskatoon berries

Wait for the blossoms—late May, June.
Five petals, white, with gaps between.
Half-finished, fragile.
Cross fingers against a late frost,
high wind, heavy rain.

Wait for the berries to fatten in July,
for red to darken into purple-blue.
Then the slow picking: from each cluster
take the two ripe ones, leave the underripe,
the shrivelled. An hour or more to fill a pail.

Wait for the mouthful of sweet purple
juice on the tongue, the almond bite
of seeds between teeth.
                                        Wait,

there's a better tree farther in.
Bigger berries.
                                        There.
The best ones are up high.
Reach for them.

Evidence

Adventurers along the river,
my brother and I jump
from rock to rock, watching
our step, watching for treasure.
We pick up signs of night's activity:
abandoned shells, their insides gone—
the lumps of flesh pried loose,
consumed. Houses unlocked,
emptied by long-fingered paws.
Clean now, smelling of river
more than mollusc. One side milky,
iridescent, the other rough,
ribbed with growth lines.
We hold them skyward, see
translucence where outer skin
is flaked away, trace little whorls,
muscle scars in the nacre.
We fill pockets with these remains
of a meal, remnants of small lives,
and leave behind footmarks
in damp sand, bent
sedges along the trail.

Image in a country church

Horse Lake, Saskatchewan

Sunday, white clapboard unbearably bright.
People shading eyes as they greet
and pass inside to hear the preacher read
the Revelation of John: *a lamb standing*
as though it had been slain—the paradox
we can hardly speak, the reason
we've come and sung, reminded again
how mystery resides in that harsh death,
the rising after, its unnerving glory. It's here
in this small clearing—that glory, declared
in morning rays through arched windows,
shining the varnished pews;
in brightness flashing out from everything:
white doors, chrome on cars, flecks of mica
in the gravelled yard. Each waxy needle on spruce,
each trembling aspen leaf, each face.

Chokecherries

You look for places where sunlight
distils to a concentrate:
interruptions in the green, dark clusters
among the oval leaves.
Taut blue-black skins holding in
juice that sucks the mouth dry.
They're big this year, you say.

It's quick work: one hand grips a stem,
the other strips off berries,
sends them plumping into the pail.
They are warm in midday heat.

At home, you rinse off the bloom of dust,
cook, strain, add sugar,
cook again. Pour thickened juice
into clear jars. Seal them.
A good batch, you say.
You label the jars, line them up
on the counter. See how the purple jelly
absorbs the light.

Park Valley

Cold February, early in Lent.
We arrive in darkness: no moon,
few yard lights pricking through the bush.

The service begins. Songs, a drama,
a sermon. Faces in the pews—
outnumbered by our visiting choir—
stare back, unmoved.

Soft chords from the reed organ:
    There is a green hill far away,
    Without a city wall,
but no one in the pews joins in.
Choir sings to the end.
Organ pedals sigh as they're released.

The churchyard is deserted as we leave,
the van's tires crunching on packed snow.
The porch light fades behind us.
If we press our faces to the windows,
we can see the stars.

Mount Carmel Shrine

Carmel, Saskatchewan

From this height we see wheat fields,
green thickets, patches of water—
everything except our children.
While we traced inscriptions
on Our Lady's plinth,
they drifted off. No interest
in *quinque lustra* or *auxilium.*

Voices rise from the north slope
and I plunge downhill, calling,
down the wide path walled in
by solid bush, a band of sky above.
Past a stone cairn with cedar cross,
plaque of hammered bronze:
Jesus is laid in the sepulchre.

The voices float ahead, indistinct.
Aspens hide the bald summit.
No cross-trails, next cairn out of sight.
I rush through stations of the cross
in reverse, circling the hill, still calling,

never coming closer. I run back
to Mary, find the children beside her.
Backward pilgrimage ended, they took
the straight road to the top. They lean
against the warm stone, laughing,
panting. Wondering where I'd gone.

Raspberries

Drops of red
among serrated leaves: the sign
you didn't know you were looking for.
Reach in, let branchfuls of prickles
scrape forearm skin. Lift
each leaf-cluster to find
the fleshy berries suspended beneath.
You don't want the pale ones
that resist when tugged off the stem,
nor the wine-red, those that fall
with the shake of a twig. Take only
the bright red, the ones that slip off
with a light fingertip grasp. These
are ready, these will burst their sacs
of juice when they pass from lips to tongue,
release sharp sweetness in the mouth.
Lean over, tip your head sideways—
with every slight shift
in your angle of vision, more
drops of red appear, until
your hands overflow.

Grid road

Canola fields pungent through rolled-down windows.
Our gaze drawn along the fence lines.

How to tell oats from barley? All grasses
generate windblown waves of light,

and one square follows another. Water interrupts.
A heron lifts off just slowly enough to show

how the blue layered on blue, the green
that follows green, are not the same.

How far can we follow the blue wingbeats?
Does the sequence of fields ever repeat?

~ Cemetery road 2 ~

Walking out from town with your brother and son, feet striking the gravel in unison, then offbeat, slipping in and out of time. The grass smells dry this summer; the little pond is only a sheet of mud. You pass along the ditch freckled with milk vetch purples. The cemetery gate arches over the driveway, steel mesh letters spelling out shadows on the ground. Your brother knows where he's headed. You and your son digress back and forth, toward whatever invites your attention: this white stone, orange lichen spreading in rough circles over an austere Celestial City; this polished black, etched with airplane and radio tower. Your brother returns from a stone in the northwest corner, the site of an old grief. Together you range back through decades, reading grey limestone obelisks, concrete pillows, slant markers in granite. A marble tablet, date of death: 1908—the oldest stone your haphazard search has discovered. Almost ninety years before your son's birth—your grandparents were children then. What else was here? Wagon tracks, pine seedlings in rows, houses small against the horizon—straight lines scratched into the landscape. You look up: against the tall hedge, a cloud of tiny flying things. A shimmer—

I used to know the place

Progress

The railway runs between fields, beside ponds,
under a warm air mass moving east. A pair
of parallel lines stitched with cross-ties.
Along it, an alphabet of settlements,
A to *Z* repeated westward. That was progress,
pushing the lines through, planting towns,
plowing up land so fast no one thought
to enumerate the wheat grass, June grass,
fescue, or knew what was lost through
the splitting of roots.

Ituna, Kelliher, Lestock: still here.
Bangor, Tate, Venn: bypassed
when the highways came through.
Elroy, Mosten, Undora: gone.

To us, watching with fresh attention,
it's all new: the glare of sun on rooftops,
sun on steel rails. This alphabet overlaid
on the landscape, its gaps written over
with field crops, wild mustard, bindweed—
foreign and local mingling on disturbed ground.
Daisies and buckbrush nodding in the train's wake.

Getaway

Two hours, maybe, just far enough to shift
from aspen parkland to spiky grass
and sandy soil—an afternoon away,
as much as time off work allows.

At a roadside picnic ground we stop,
pull out ball and glove, Frisbee, cooler chest.
Cloth to cover the table's peeling paint
and graffiti. In the chest, tuna sandwiches,
fresh-picked lettuce, radishes, iced tea.
Chocolate cookies iced with vanilla.

Wild roses fill the ditch, flat
pink blossoms sweet
and soft as talc.
I wade in for a sniff,
mingle their scent with dust
kicked up from tall grass.

It's possible to know there's more
and not want it. It's possible for this
to be enough: the cottonwoods'
dry patter, and underneath it
our voices (small, without echo);
a meadowlark, a killdeer;
the approach and retreat of a single car.

Gabriel's Crossing

My brother followed me, climbing
the riverbank's cut-open face,
slipping, kicking back sand-spurts.
We slid down, scrambled up,
slithered and tumbled till feet,
hands, clothes were sand-brown.
The hillside concave, grass
and wild roses stripped away,
truckloads hauled off for road work,
there by the sky-blue bridge
near the place where Dumont ran the ferry.

At school it was Radisson, not Riel;
Vimy, not Fish Creek. Batoche was
a Sunday outing—graveyard, rifle pits,
bullet holes in clapboard. Battles
with losses we could not fathom.

We pronounced *Gabriel* as if it were English.
We raided the riverbank to fill our sandbox.

Halfway up

The hill was steeper than I remembered,
grown over with grass, wild roses, willows.
Up the middle of a small fold
in the riverbank, a trail
scraped clear of cover, bare sand
smooth and hot underfoot.
I was there yesterday, to see
whether the place still matched
the pictures in my mind.

Returning now
in my sleep, once again climbing
beside the sand trail, where vegetation
holds the earth together. I grasp
at shrubs, lean into the slope.
Hoping to reach, again, the level place
halfway up, where I can turn,
stand upright, take in the river's
long sweep, catch a breath.

I raise my head and see,
not far above, a lynx's tufted ears
and white-tipped fur. What stops me
is not fear, but puzzlement:
how it can lie curled up on the slope;
how it looks at me, yet seems
to be asleep.

It rises, slips away
as quick as thought. I try
to photograph its tracks,
clear prints stamped in dry sand.
These, too, disappear.
I'm left searching for what
could not possibly be there.
Marks of claws. Green eyes
reflecting light.

Lanigan Creek revisited

Down the slope from the road, waist-deep
in cow parsnip. Thistles rasp my bare legs.
Down farther, in black currant and nettle,
I don't see the horseflies till they bite.

Reeds grow thick along the creek
where it widens to a pond.
Two killdeer run across the mudflat
fringed with green scum.

Behind me, a plastic lid flotilla,
chip bags, a Slurpee cup wash against
a concavity of shoreline.
These things did not appear
within the frame of memory,
but they're here now, like
the loud ones at the party
(everyone looking sideways,
asking who let *them* in).

I keep my eyes on the birds,
their stop-and-start progress across
the shining mud. No need for them
to raise their *kill-dee* alarm call;
I'm hemmed in by reeds and willow,
far enough away.

Pin cherries

We headed east from town on the old highway.
My mother knew, somehow, which dirt trail
at the edge of someone's farmland
was the one. The car rubbed its belly
on the grassy hump between the ruts,
branches slapping its sides.

They were never as abundant
as the chokecherries, but
my mother knew where to look:
open spaces, where full sun
freckled the bushes with scarlet.
We picked them into plastic honey pots
slung by shoelaces around our necks.

Later, they somehow turned to jelly,
bright as the tiny cherries, glossy
on the knife tip. Eaten after school
in the kitchen, cool and tart on a fresh bun.

But that was years ago, where
we used to live. This place must lack
something pin cherries need to thrive.
My mother only says, *No,*
I've never found any around here.

Near Petrofka Bridge

I used to know the place.
West of town, across the bridge, turn right and

then what? Down this trail, I think.
Down, then up toward the clearing
where we sat around tables and barbecue pits
and the aunts opened Tupperware filled with
sandwiches, devilled eggs, puffed wheat squares.
An occasion. A rare visit from Ontario cousins,
caught in square snapshots from a pocket camera.

There's nothing here now.

It's dusk, beginning to snow.
Too cold to stand around, too dark to see
where the ground drops away
toward the river. I walk back,
wary of gopher holes, to where
I think I left the car.

Not here.

Trees melt into clouded sky
in the growing dark. I stumble
through a hollow in the grass, then
feel gravel underfoot. The road bends,
bush thins out, and there's the car,
a strange shape in the deep indigo.

Retreat

On the balcony, coffee before breakfast.
A circle talking politics mingled
with family news. Mist rises from the folds
of riverbank unwinding northward.
Someone asks, *What's happened with the spill?*
Someone says, *The oil company's got four,*
five hundred hired to clean it up.
Others nod, tip mugs to their lips.
One murmurs into his coffee,
Hope they know what they're doing.

It's this river, the one we see
through thinning mist.
Later, we walk down to the edge.
We swam here once, in the slow-flowing
channel by the island.
Was the water always murky like this?
Those odd swirls on the surface,
were they there before?
We think it must look different, but—
five years since we saw this place—
how do we know?
A sign at the dock warns: DO NOT GO IN.

The Fort revisited

What we're seeing is really sky.
It retreats as we approach.

The road's heat rises. Light bends.
The riverbank blue in the distance.

~

Into the valley, the woods breathing coolness.
This was always a *here*,

crossroads of water and land routes
in a mosaic of aspen and fescue.

Rebellion or Resistance?
The steep drop on our left, hidden by trees.

~

The notched edge of the palisade: upright logs
chisel-tipped like beavers' tooth-work.

This catwalk didn't feel so dangerous
when our shoulders barely cleared the railing.

~

The way to tell new wood from old is by smell.
Upstairs in the fur store: dusty heat.

Reconstructions. Outlines of what once was.
Swallows rest in the shade of a chimney.

Bearings

Rural Municipality of Usborne

51° 45' 41" North, 105° 08' 53" West.
Rail lines cut across its corners,
routes that once led the way to
    Your Own Farm In Canada
    The Right Land for the Right Man.
Roads and fences subdividing
smaller and smaller squares, creeks
winding their own way regardless—
these are the visible lines.

                        The invisible:
range and township boundaries.
Official lines that mark
responsibility for firefighting,
flood protection, pest control.
The long curve, following rivers
and streams northeast to southwest,
that divides Treaty 6 from Treaty 4
(you might not know this
without asking, and you might
not ask till someone tells you).

In the *Atlas of Saskatchewan*, this tract of land
lies between boreal and prairie, within
a tea-green band running southeast, the aspen parkland
this once was. Still is. Except—on another page,
Landsat image shows a wash of champagne-
yellow cropland. Chartreuse grassland
in shreds and patches, spots
of midnight-blue marsh.
Woodlands, olive-green
specks, indistinct.

Page further—
the settlement map is a Tetris of coloured
blocks. Pale blue for Mennonites, dark
for German Lutherans. Rose for the little
Irish colony, red for the few Norwegians.
For "Indian Reserves," the palest almost-pink.
Against the surrounding colours, it almost disappears.

Wild strawberries

Wind sways the tall caraganas
that line the graveyard's boundary,
tosses the crowns of pine trees
set in straight rows down the middle.
High above our heads, a crow calls.

                    When we crouch low
among the stones, pinpoints of colour
become violets, yellow cinquefoil.
Toothed leaves, brushed aside, reveal
bright berries. We lie together in the tangle
of grass and tiny flowers, eat strawberries,
tell stories of these people who died
before our time. We stay close
to the ground, so the wind
will not blow us away.

~ Cemetery road 3 ~

Walking this road in winter for the first time. The road is the same, maybe emptier. Winter is as winter always is: snow painfully bright under clear sky. It's deep on the fields this year, none of the gold stubble showing. You cast a blue shadow, drawn long in front of you. The bare willows are red even now. You pull your hood up; the wind is sharp. The lane into the cemetery's drifted shut. You step onto the crust of snow and it holds you up. Farther in, between the rows of pines, it's not so deep. Footprints, some sort of canine—wild, maybe, since the only human prints are yours. Signs of a struggle: smaller prints, a confusion of tracks, blurry trail leading away. You try to trace the sequence of events, map this incident that was probably over in moments. The prints cross each other, overlap, disappear. You pull a scrap of paper from your pocket, outline toes, claws—no detail; it's too cold for bare hands. Paper stuffed back into pocket, hands into mittens. Turning back toward the gate, you pick your way around the paw prints, wanting to leave them undamaged. For whose benefit, you couldn't say.

Omand's Creek

Open arms

April

Welcome the warbler, the mourning dove,
startled wings rising from footpaths.
Welcome the prelude to leaves, red
stamens clustered on maples.

Welcome the footbridge rising from water,
the creek receding, fish odour of mud.

Welcome wind flipping the song sparrow's
feathers, rocking grey branches.
Welcome the bird's uptilted head,
its throat-pulsing stutter, staccato.

Welcome snow's final retreat
that lays everything bare: blue
Pepsi cup, green plastic bag
stark against dead grass,
a call to repentance.

Affirmation

May

The slopes are dull as pavement,
creek's edge dry with last year's cattails.
Coffee cups, bright red faded to brick,
lodge in bushes. Windblown fast-food logos,
disguised by dirt and sun-bleach,
entangle in the yellowed grass.

Step sideways—the picture changes.
New grass threading up through the old,
willow twigs bursting with leaves, rosehips
still orange after winter, the advertisement
of a blackbird's scarlet shoulders.

Tomorrow, neighbours will come
with gloves and garbage bags, kick up dust
from blades of bluestem. They'll comb out
the cardboard and plastic that's drifted in.
Push back the boundaries yet again.

Plenty

June

On each stalk, a whorl of long-toothed leaves
and a white, round-petalled flower. Single,
but not alone: lateral stems underground—
an unbroken connection—multiply anemones
one to two, to four, a family, a clan
inhabiting the moist shade by the creek.

On the crest of the bank under sun,
rose bushes bristle together—a pretty tight crowd,
but open-handed with their pink blooms,
their size, their sweetness. Enough for all
the pollen-gatherers, with basketfuls to spare.

Downstream, milk vetch throng beside the path.
One taproot grows a multitude, narrow leaflets
twinning down each long stalk. Flower stems
add purple to purple: finger-flicks
of colour, little J-strokes, climb each other
up and up, heaping plenty on plenty
in this extravagant season.

Come closer

July

The gaillardia, those yellow-red suns,
pulled you aside. What made you stay:
purples, every shade you could wish for—
pale to bright, lilac to magenta.
And white, in more patterns and forms
than you ever knew: half-bald heads
of prairie clover; Culver's root,
spikes of tight-lipped blooms;
everlastings in cat's-paw clusters;
yarrow canopies; milkweed stars.

Step closer. Slip between
the flowering stalks, cup their faces
in your hand, rub a leaf between your fingers—
scent of orange peel, cool sage, vanilla,
honey cakes. Touch the point of each petal.
Sun's warm on your neck.
Why return to the path?
Where else would you go?

Invasive species

August

Dragged out of its habitat, abandoned,
it found the downward slope and kept rolling.
Now it's half-swallowed in silt, greened over
with slippery fronds, smartweed sprouting
between immobilized wheels. Its handle,
lettered red and white to show where
it belongs, now tilts into the creek.

Still, this one's not as bad as those two
under the bridge, mud-spattered,
gone mad with rust. This one's
steel frame is stainless, polished
in flowing water. Its wheels,
cleaned up a little, might still spin.

Catfish nose their way between the bars
of its open cage, slip on downstream.
The thing will stay, sinking deeper in
the creek bed, its angles never softening,
a snag for someone's fishing line.
Time will pass like water.

Equinox

September

Summer empties its paint pots.
A drip here, a splash there: vermilion
on white, chartreuse on brown.
Gold-burst. Final glory of purple.

The passage between seasons is the breadth
of the creek bank. Up by the train tracks,
asters line the wire fence, each flower
with half its petals fresh, half faded.
Four blooms on a thistle: two stiff,
two soft as fur. Seed pods of milkweed
show permutations of open or closed,
beige or celadon, white-woolly seeds clinging
or windblown.

                    Amid flaming rose leaves,
spikes of giant hyssop stand dark and petalless.
But even these dead ones aren't dead:
at the base of a dry stem, two leaves remain.
In the bald seed head, a scent.

Dwindling

October

Green to gold, gold to dun. A drying
and stripping-down, slow but sure unleaving.
Not much remains now: faded grass,
goldenrod gone to seed, a scatter
of blue-violet stars along the path.
Everlastings, their spiky white petals
clustered on naked stems. Dogwood
and rose leaves, red and red.
The cranberry smell of the woods.
The alien gleam from two black
bags, filled and tied, pushed under
a shrub. The great and small
of bristled things: burdock thicket,
head-high; wild licorice, brown
and stiff among the grass.
And milkweed husks with tips
to prick a finger on, brittle,
their thistledown flown.

Not yet

November

Early on, the cattail stalks
keep the last of their green,
the creek ice only a skin.
Now, deep into November,
it's three fingers thick at the breach
in the beaver dam. Flowing water
uncoils from the gap in a thin rope,
frost-needles along its edge.
On the bank, a maple trunk
with scrape marks from
squared-off incisors;
saplings harvested with clean,
diagonal cuts; a chiselled stump.
The beavers holed up, or moved on,
because it's cold now—
not like the worst of winter,
but sharp enough to mask
the tinge of plant-smell,
vestige of autumn overripeness
that was already almost gone.
A skiff of snow presses
dried flower heads and grass blades
toward the ground. A weight,
but not a covering. Not yet.

Secrets

December

Upstream on snow-covered ice,
the willows within arm's reach
on either side. Easiest way to travel
this stretch of the creek—its banks
pathless here, thick with tall grass,
shrubby maples, and sow thistle.
Its corridor narrowed, train tracks
on one side, steakhouse on the other.
Small mysteries here: halfway
to the bend, the creek steps up,
the reason (rocks? a beaver dam?)
anonymous under snow.
Farther on, broken-off posts
from a structure long fallen to ruin.
But where the stream curves
and the tracks cross over, too much
is revealed—graffiti glaring
from bridge piers, concrete flaked
and cracked, rebar skeleton exposed—
so that you nearly miss, just here
where wind sweeps the ice almost clean,
faint marks of hooves and paws.

Constraint

January

Farther upstream, near Garbage Hill,
a nondescript retail block extends
its parking lot, held up by concrete pilings,
over the creek. Hardly room here
for left and right banks: Empress Street
a curb on one side, on the other
a succession of paint shop,
vape shop, auto parts, Walmart,
parking lot, beer store, hardware,
parking lot. Excavators, perched
halfway down the slope, dig out
curls of black clay, fill holes with
crushed rock, tamp it down. This
is what the creek has to get through
between city limits and that last stretch—
the small patch of restored prairie,
the woods, the ravine—where it's allowed
to meander again.

Distant/close

February

The sun's muted today, screened
behind sheer cloud, ringed with a faint
halo. From down here on the creek,
the horizon's just overhead.

A few cars, a bus, a van pass by.
Their sound skims past overhead,
their wheels invisible.

Down here there's a fitful wind, slight
there-and-gone rustle in the cattails.
Trampled snow that squeaks underfoot,
untrodden snow that sinks with a *whumf*
under each footfall. This morning's dusting
that blurs yesterday's squirrel tracks.

Distant traffic, a shapeless hum:
sometimes insistent,
more often retreating behind the quiet.

No birds down here today.
Each nest capped with snow.

Alert

March

Coming through the woods, the water
runs fast and yellow-brown.
Getting ahead of itself: below this thin,
swift current, the ice lies thick.
But the sun's angle is shifting;
it's warm on the white ground.
Where maples and wild plums thin out,
willows cluster by the stream,
fine lines like hairs on end,
the rust-orange of squirrel fur,
bristled, alert:
what is it   *what*
is it   *spring*
is it?

You, too, watch for signs
of what's coming. You listen hard
for the sound of meltwater, wait to be told
how to love the world.

~ Cemetery road 4 ~

Too early to be certain, but as you turn onto the road, it's there—a scent of change, faint odour of melting, a fleeting sensation in your nostrils. Still, once you head north, the breeze is keen enough to make your face tingle. Just ahead, a magpie flaps over the road in a low arc, from willows on the left to poplars on the right, calling *yeck-yeck-yeck*. High above, there's a muted airplane hum, but nothing in sight. After a moment you spot it, a tiny white cutout moving east, its sound lagging behind. That's all—no vapour trail, no interrupting cloud. The sky bright, but not glaring. Snow pillows around bent grasses in the ditch. Distant trees, grey-limbed, bristle like fur. You're aware their softness will stiffen as you come nearer—all the same, you want to keep walking till you reach them. Not because of the trees themselves, but to stay in this instant of wide-awakeness, this intimation that you've just walked through a doorway in the air. And yet there's a pull to go back, a feeling you're needed at home, more than before. A little farther, to where the paved surface ends and gravel begins, then you turn and walk toward town. Steam rises from puddles on the asphalt. The words in your head dissolve, leaving you strangely content. Lightened.

Blue hills

Breathless

Crossing the prairie by bus was nothing
compared to that 747—two aisles, six galleys,
the long, long line on the viewscreen map,
the hours of sleep it takes
to cross an ocean and a continent.
Breathless as when I left home
for the first time, and far more
aware of how little it came to, the sum
of my second-hand knowing.
At thirty-five thousand feet,
what I knew shrank down to
a TV image recalled from childhood:
news anchor at his desk, map
displayed behind him, the name
Phnom Penh beside a dot.

But knowing coconuts grow
on trees is not the same
as tipping a fresh one to your mouth
and drinking its sweet juice.
They told me Cambodia is
hot and dusty; now the heat
drags on my limbs, pale dust sticks
to my sunscreened neck.
They did not describe how it feels,
being too white to fade into a crowd,
learning to be stared at.
Or how the sugar palms look
from the back of a motorbike.
Their silhouettes against blue hills.

Barefoot girls

The Khmer word for art, silapak, *in fact, at its root, means "magic."*—Prumsodun Ok

I've no idea what they'll do when the music starts,
this troupe from the fine arts school
in loose trousers, royal blue,
their flat chests buttoned into tight blouses.
Shoulders down and back, necks straight,
faces composed. Ready.

It's a slow rolling of heel to toe,
knees bent, feet flexed. It's the arc
of their spines. A sinuous line,
a wave without climax or end.

And it's their improbable hands,
their backward-curving fingers,
alphabet of slow gestures:
tree, leaf, flower, fruit.

Now each girl holds a bowl of white petals.
They dance for all visitors to this park,
and today I'm the only one.
Captured by their slight smiles,
the water-flow of their steps,
the petals they scatter.

What they do here

Cyclo, madame?
No, thank you.

I walk. Early, when the heat still
lies in wait behind the sweet
magnolia breath, the dust,
the vegetative damp. Before the air's
too thick to wade through.
Never fast or far.

Cyclo, madame?
No, thank you.

Why you always walk,
madame? You walk,
you get tired!

Yes—but this is what I know,
how I feel my way through
unfamiliar places.

Still, why not
admit I'm wilting, nestle into
the bucket seat slung between
two gently squeaking wheels,
lean back under the sunshade,
and let this wiry old man
thread his slow way through
the traffic? Why not just ride?
It's what they do here.

Ratana takes me to the market

She helps me barter for a length of silk,
sapphire blue shot with purple.
Enough for two skirts, says the woman in the stall.
I buy the silk, two scarves, a silver spoon;
ignore the shoes and jewellery, the pirated videos.

A merchant squatting on the ground
sells little black things from a basket.
Ratana tells me they are crickets
stuffed with peanuts and fried.
In the Pol Pot time, she says,
when her family had so little to eat,
they sometimes caught crickets or lizards.
She doesn't eat crickets now.

I can think of nothing to say to this.
I remember the lizard yesterday,
skittering through grass
by a temple wall. Barely a glimpse
of legs and twitching tail,
and it was gone.

Tuol Sleng

Schoolgirls in navy and white
follow me.
One of them giggles.

In the bare room, an iron bed,
shackles, chains.
Photo on the wall verifies
the bloodstain on the floor.

The girls watch
as I move slowly
through each room.
When I reach the second building,
they're gone.

Here the space narrows,
classrooms divide into cells
one metre by two.

Upstairs it's empty.
A painted number marks each iron ring
screwed into concrete walls.

And then this room.

Three broken Buddhas. A wooden chest
without a cover, painted green.
Full of bones.

Vesak Day in Tram Kak

The temple is new, paint still fresh
on walls where giant figures
play out stories of the Buddha—
birth, enlightenment, death—
under cool fluorescents flecked
with bugs. We sit behind the nuns
all in white, grey hair cut short.
Monks in orange-yellow robes,
some of them just boys, watch us
and smile behind their hands.
They'll stay here all night.
This is what I was told.
Also, the reason the old nuns
grin at me: the great joke
of my being here, winter-pale,
not understanding a word.

Buddha looks down from his dais,
pink and smiling, mounds of flowers
at his feet. Boy-monks fidget and stare,
the women sip jasmine tea
as the sermon drones to an end.
Musicians wait with practised stillness,
sitting behind xylophones, a circle
of gong chimes, stout barrel of a drum.
One of them—a blind man, grey-haired
and hollow-cheeked—lets a few notes loose.

A brief measure and he stops, mallets raised,
mumbling his cigarette. Then the signal—
whatever it is—comes for real.
They all catch it, pick up their sticks,
wait a beat, and begin.

Waking in Angk Ta Saom

Everything's monochrome,
silver-blue with moonlight:

the wooden house on stilts,
windows shut against mosquitoes;

the wash house with palm-leaf walls
and clay water jar, the latrine out back;

the two pigs lying together,
snuffling in their sleep.

I crawl out of pink mosquito netting,
slip on sandals, pad along the dirt path,

open the door to a squat toilet
in spotless white tile.

One pig twitches an ear.

If I stand very still,
there's a possibility
of a breeze.

Bakong

Children climb thousand-year-old steps,
young men walk the temple's high terraces.

The tower at its summit, small and dim inside.
Fresh incense and waxy lotus blooms.

A modern temple just outside the ancient walls,
the conversation between old and new

carried on in constant footsteps.
A funeral and a celebration:

a hearse, strung with tiny lights;
new monks, a gathering in saffron.

The children in their white shirts, fresh from school.
Women in jewel-bright sarongs.

Incense and keening music.
Sticky rice and cans of Coke for sale.

The hearse painted gold and red.
Sarongs embroidered in gold.

Bright on grey. Silk on stone.
Air quivering with heat.

Market in Siem Reap

Mangosteen
Colour of an eggplant, but not as shiny.
Shape of a tomato, but not soft.
Rind hard as a melon's, but not so thick.
Segments like an orange, but no membranes.
Juicy like a peach, but sweeter.
Flesh white like nothing else.

Durian
Delicacy—now there's a word
to arouse suspicion.
Oblong, brown, spiny. Open it up:
no juice drips out. Soft insides,
yellow, stinking of old fish,
rotten eggs, and skunk.

Mango
Cut it open like this: lengthwise here—
and here—to remove the flat seed.
Criss-cross the knife through each half,
turn the skin inside out, bite off
chunks of bright flesh. Let the juice
sugar-coat your wrists.

Rambutan
Scraggly-haired creatures, red-faced,
hang from a twig. Crack their skins,
pop out the slippery globule.
Try to bite. The surface resists.
You have to take it in whole.

After

Fresh fish at the ByWard Market—a flash-
back to Phnom Penh.

Ginger chicken at home, not quite like
the restaurant's on Sisowath Quay.

A dress made of the silk
Ratana helped me buy.

Arriving home is dizzying.
I'm waiting to catch up with myself.

Pictures. A 500-riel note.
A beer bottle: Angkor Extra Stout.
What else?

On sale at the Rideau Centre,
a cardigan, pale blue with shell buttons:
Made in Cambodia/Fabriqué au Cambodge.

News report says Pol Pot may be dead.
News report confirms Pol Pot is dead.
There is no more news.

Silk

Diamonds set in sapphire,
outlines blurred as if in motion
or out of focus (from the shifting
of threads during weaving).
Border of crosses and dots,
wavering white line along the selvage.

The woman in the market stall
swishing her hands to show
the silk is washable.

Tie-dyed weft builds the design,
purple warp strands invisible
on the front side, shimmering
on the back of the fabric, bright
along the raw edges.

I unfold thin paper templates,
pin and cut. Straight bodice,
gathered skirt—not the way
Khmer women wear it.
I don't have that pattern.

Front and back pinned together,
sliding under the presser foot.
Straight stitch the seams, zigzag
the edges to keep them
from fraying.

I clip the stray threads.
Slip into blue.
My small, imperfect map.

~ Cemetery road 5 ~

Even the narrow stand of bush edging the cemetery could hold all kinds of life—things you have no idea of. But rarely do you see chipmunk stripes, or a flicker's spotted belly. Most often there's only a small sound, or the after-echo of a sound just missed—a signal you've come very close to a creature that wants no part of you. A question that holds you in place. Once, in the town south of here, a woman saw a cougar from her kitchen window. You learned, then, that cougars are solitary and secretive; you could have one living nearby and never know it. And once, riding the train through the Qu'Appelle Valley, you heard a voice over the speakers: *Ladies and gentlemen, on your left, a moose.* You turned, and saw only the hillside. So now, standing near the invasive caraganas that divide the mowed grass from the bush—quiet enough to hear the *tick* of their seed pods opening—you're prepared to believe anything could live here. Like in that Dr. Seuss book about the boy fishing in the pool that just might connect to an underground river and then to the sea, home to unheard-of wonders that might swim upstream to be caught. But you have no hopes of catching anything that lives in this bush. Maybe a glimpse of a small face. And even that sometimes seems too great a thing to ask for.

~ Cemetery road 6 ~

Just off this road, along the old highway that crosses it, the bush grows right to the fence. You went out there with your brother once. No PRIVATE PROPERTY sign, or none that you could see, and an opening that looked like a path. You turned, crossed the ditch, went a little way in. Pushed branches aside, releasing them slowly so as not to snap each other's faces. One of you saw the deer and alerted the other with a touch. You stood still, breathing as shallowly as you could, watching the deer as it looked at you. It stood across your path, its head turned toward you. Closer than you'd ever been to such wildness without a fence to separate. For a long moment, nothing moved. Then, responding to a signal you couldn't detect, the deer let out its breath with a *whuff*, and before you could say *Wait, don't—* it leaped away, further into the bush, out of sight. After that, the landowner put up NO TRESPASSING signs along the fence. And like the obliging people you are, you and your brother left the bush alone, though you looked toward it every time you passed that way. Whatever went on among those trees went on, free and secret, as it had always done.

Settling into motion

On our own

Almost midnight, with faint stars
and a quarter moon. I press my face
to the coach window, cup hands around
my eyes. Headlights wait at a crossing.
A yard light outlines a house and barn.

I sit back, let my reflection appear.
My hair's just long enough to braid.
I gather the top strands, divide in three,
cross over and under. My window-self
also has hands poised behind her head.
I can't see what her hands, or mine,
are doing, but soon the French braid's
done. Lumpy in places, but it'll hold.

When my grandma rode the train for days
and nights westward from the port, she had
her mother and three sisters with her.
They could inspect each other's hair,
make sure the braids were tight and smooth
all the way down. She was twenty then,
and wore her braids pinned up.
Unpinned, they reached her waist.

Window-girl and I look at each other.
This is the first time we've done it
on our own. We turn our heads, check
each other's handiwork as best we can.

All this light

1.

I spent extra for a lower berth
just for the window. So now,
curtained in, half undressed,
I resist sleep for the sake of this
moonlight trail across hard-polished snow,
the way it travels with the train, the way
I'm always looking along a straight line
from window to moon.

An old ritual revived. My teenaged self,
in bed in the small green room upstairs,
pulled back the curtain every night
for one last look before lights-out.
Couldn't say why, except that
doing it once meant doing it always.

Past midnight now, my eyes gritty with fatigue.
When fields give way to forest, when the chain
of moonlight breaks, then I'll sleep.

2.

Waiting to depart. Awake at midnight,
head against the window, rolled-up sweater
prickling my cheek. Still in the station,
in the dark, on a silent train. Hardly a rustle
from other seats. Now and then
a head leans into the aisle, listening
for any signal, any news.

Lights go on abruptly, engine hums.
One jolt and we're moving. I sleep again
and wake with my eyes full
of sun. The other passengers
lower their blinds. An attendant
strolls in, swinging long arms
in too-short sleeves. *Last call,*
he says. *Last call for breakfast*
in the dining car. No one gets up.

Snowdrifts and sun. I blink,
close my eyes. Unsure what to do
with all this light.

Thirty-day pass

1. Departure

This is your final call.
Rush through the echoing rotunda,
tramping on maple leaves inlaid in the floor.
Backpacks bounce on our shoulders.
All passengers should now be on board.

Shock of sunlight as the train leaves the station,
escapes the city, picks up speed.
You try out camera buttons,
I stare across sunflower fields.
We are farther east than we've ever been.
We hear there are lakes upon lakes; we hear
of Mud River, Hornepayne, Washago.
Red River behind us, we watch,
ready to catch with a *Look!*
and shutter click.
Over and over,
all the way to the coast.

2. Seen

Lake, trees, rock, trees, lake.
Trees. Water giving back sky's blue,
doubled. Trees, rock, trees again,
a lake.

Black things in a bog: bare
trunks tilting. A bear.

Tamarack, tamarack, spruce.
Red pine, Jack pine, white pine.
(*For you I pine, for you I balsam.*)

Church spire, mist, a hill of trees.
Rocks on a windy lake.

The train's long S slipping through
the pine   spruce
    fir   tamarack   pine

3. Two nights and a day

Tree and lake and tree flow through our sleep.
We wake to a forest changed,
an increase of oak and aspen among the pines.
We doze again, lulled by rock and water,
by shade and dapple of green passing and passing.
Doze and wake, sway down the aisle to the snack bar.
Nothing left but candy and withered apples.

Forest dwindles. We scarcely see the change—
you curled into yourself, my legs draped over an armrest.
Brick farmhouses pass in a blink. Pavement spreads,
beige subdivision closes in around us.
We've forgotten how to use our limbs.
We can hardly raise our heads.

4. Ontario

We're going to fall into the lake.
I say this aloud, unprepared
for the size of it, so close.
The far shore's invisible, a thread
dividing blue from blue.

You lean toward the window.
No, you say, *there's ground*
between us and the water.
Look.
          I don't want to.
The train stays on the tracks,
you know, you say with a laugh,
and I make myself look,
just to show you.

The man across the aisle
stares out the window too,
eyes half shut, saying nothing.
Drinking a beer slowly. Then another.
When the cart comes again he says, *Well,*
we don't have lakes like this in England,
and orders two more.

5. Over and over

passing through stands of poplar
shadow-stripes   lightdarklightdark

conductor strides through the coach
calls for the steward   *François! François!*

the train lurches leftright as I walk
down the aisle for water

black-haired boys kick and wriggle
poke poke and grin
when their sister wails

their father sleepless unshaven
lays bologna on margarine on bread
for each and each

I sit again   eyes flitting
book to aisle to window

paperback pages flip
flip

6. Halifax

White spars along the pier,
HMCS Sackville stamped on a gangway,
blue-and-white flags on masts
sun-bright against the little clouds.
And there, a ship—a cargo ship
approaching, containers stacked
red and white on its deck
white   green   red   blue
stacked four and five high. A ship
bigger than twenty boxcars, bigger
than all the houses in town.
We capture it, click after click—
front half, rear, full view   click again—
the photos will all look the same
but we keep cameras pointed
at the ship passing the pier,
the fistful of pictures firm evidence:
we were definitely here.

Chance

Tea in a dark-green tin: bergamot scent of Earl Grey
with something more, a hint of smoke.

That's the one. The tea from the train
to Moncton—remember?—where we met
the musician, that long-legged clarinetist,
blond bangs falling in his eyes, who chattered
about symphonies and shoes and England,
who shook his hair aside and offered us tea,
a dark-green box pulled from his pack,
who beckoned us along to fetch hot water
(matching our stride to the coach's rocking)

—one whiff

of smoky bergamot and it's present again,
that eastward trip with you: settling into motion,
hefting backpacks down from luggage racks,
first glimpse of coastline and ocean blue,
wandering new streets in search of sandwiches
and a laundromat—not the things we kept
and called souvenirs, but those that slipped
into memory's inner pocket, where only chance
could find them.

In the dome car

We should have passed this way hours ago
with daylight enough to see the Qu'Appelle River
slip by, loop after loop—light enough to tell
the shape on the opposite ridge is a potash mine,
to tell that grass is green, cattle are black.
Instead, the crowd in the dome car watches
sunset flood the horizon with colour
while everything else grows dim.
The man heading to see his grandchild
is here—two hours, he says, down gravel roads
to board the train before dawn—
and the young Swiss woman, wondering if
what she's been told about grain elevators
is true (people, she says, will tell you anything).
There's the man with the zoom lens,
who's been clicking shutter-bursts—
kshkshksh—all evening; the Riders fan
in his green jersey, who's heard it all before;
his friend with the basset-hound eyes.
And the sixtyish woman with turquoise hair,
travelling a month in coach,
who comes up here every dawn and dusk.
The river gives off sky-light for a while,
then fades. The red gets redder until
it goes. *That's a farm down there,*
I tell her, *that single light.* She nods
as if she almost believes me.

Probability

9 a.m., none in sight; 10:30 on the train,
gaining speed through August countryside,
it's the whether-or-not of clouds, a fleet
sailing in from the east, shadowing fields
of ripening barley. Solid mass on the horizon
separates into tufts, a field's breadth between,
coming and coming toward us, and we toward them.
Probability of rain, yes or no? To the northeast,
nimbostratus the colour of denim, ready
to wring itself out over clustered rooftops,
over the square church, onion-domed,
backlit against the oncoming storm.
But here, we're still patching our way
through sun and shade, the high/low
of small clouds: bright white and sunlit
above; below, dust-coloured, riding heavy
over sloughs. A pelican's feathers
cloud over, then clear. In the window seat,
I open my book and squint
in the sudden glare on the page.

Stopped in the Qu'Appelle Valley

A wind-ripple crosses the grass on the slope.
In the folds of hills, trees lean over, flash
their leaves' pale undersides. From this distance,
your hand is big enough to cover the terrain
almost to the lip of the valley. You hold your palm
in front of the window, wave it lightly
back and forth, riffling the grass as if it were
your kid's hair, or fur on a rabbit's back.
If this were a story, the kind you loved
as a child, what you'd do right now is walk
down the aisle of the coach, through the door
toward the dining car, but in the vestibule
you'd turn instead, and open the door
to the outside (you'd know how
to pick the lock). Maybe you'd stumble
when you hit the ground. Probably
you'd tear your shirt on the barbed-wire fence
as you spread the strands apart, bent double,
and stepped through. Seed heads of wheatgrass
would brush your calves, leaf edges a tickle
on your skin. With each step up the slope—
feet tilting over tussocks, through hollows—
you'd shrink into the landscape, no taller
than a thistle. Panting, pulse quickening,
you'd climb until you finally found
your other self—the brave one, the adventurer,
up there amid the aspen shadows—
who's been waiting for you all these years.

~ Cemetery road 7 ~

Walking in the afternoon, the sun still high. Almost too hot to be out, exposed to the blaze. Green and blue all around, but all you can think of is gold, the way things give off light: quartz and mica flecks in the gravel, a bird's wing, a waterweed, a beetle's carapace. The surface of the little pond is blinding. Hardly a pond, only a water-filled ditch, but enough to hold the sun and flash it back, hard. From a distance, the cemetery's a darkness of trees. You pass through the gate, and inside it's dazzling. Light leaps the tall hedge, shines off granite, off minuscule marble facets. You place a hand on a white stone, a red, a black, feel how they gather the heat. You've waited for this midsummer, have always loved it, despite days like this when the heat is too much. You step into shade, under a maple. Even here, looking out from this shelter, the light's so strong you can drink it.

~ **Cemetery road 8** ~

Silver and gold: wolf willow next to goldenrod, thistledown among foxtails dotting the edge of the field. Butterflies, the ever-present cabbage whites, a pair spiralling around each other, rising higher over the dusty gravel, and below them a single yellow sulphur—just one, in rapid, purposeful flight across the road toward the alfalfa, its yellow wings bordered in black. All this open space around, and your gaze fastens on those wings, thinner than a leaf. And when you reach the cemetery and wander among stones, what claims your attention amid that whole expanse is the little wood frog, its body the size of your thumb. If it hadn't moved just when you looked down, you would have missed it. What keeps you there, bent low over grass, is the fine white streak below its black eye mask, and the movement of its breathing, quick and sharp, its sides bulging and deflating. And the silver sheen on its skin.

Resisting the return to shore

Thanks

For clear October, a stiff west wind.
For the shoreline, green and gold.
For balsam poplar, balsam fir, spruce, birch, and alder.
For the boathouse, row of cabins, upside-down canoes.
For the new chapel, a solid square embraced by trees.
For our voices under its rafters.
For smell of pine in thick beams and trusses.
For young carpenters who fitted and framed.
For roofing finished before the snow.
For all that's left to do.
For the newness of the lake through these windows.
For how we count time by our returning here.

Here

Here's where the poplar fell in the storm.
That's where hard rain gouged the road.
This is the way up the hill.

That's the last of the old cabins—see the moss on the roof?
Somewhere in here there's poison ivy.
Wild iris and pond lily—there, and there.

Here's the island we sometimes swim to.
That way, the peninsula that looks like an island.
Farther yet, remains of a gold mine we've never seen.

That's the rock where the heron stood.
Here, the deer saw itself in the window.
There, the fox passed by on the road.

My family came here because of someone,
who came because of someone else,
and so on, back to a beginning.

This is the tamarack we planted.
These are the spaces in our midst.
This is where we gather in the evenings.

Timelines

A brief rasp of aluminum on basalt
as we pull up the canoe. Then nothing
except our footsteps: tapping on rock,
muffled in springing moss, rustling
through carpet of bunchberry.

It's always quiet at the field station
just up the shore, the students
spending days up on some outcrop
learning to read these lavas and sediments,
their ancient shifts and collisions.

Beside us, the centerpiece of this alcove
in the cliff: the lichen-crusted slab
that once slid down the rock face
and now leans against it, leaving
a keyhole slit we can't slip through.
High up, a black spruce grips a ledge,
somehow finds space for roots.

Voices ping off the water—the children
and teenagers arriving in two canoes.
Straight to the cliff once they disembark,
and in moments one of them finds a path,
a steep zigzag up its fractured face.
She perches among ferns, bright
against the old, old rocks.

Unfolding

The dock spider extends a leg,
then another. Emerges from under a leaf, watches
her thousand spiderlings netted in silk.

Minnowing

They school in the shallows, their slips
of shadow following beneath,
the lake bottom rippling in sandy waves.
When they idle in the water, I reach
for the long-handled net, let it swish
toward them, then watch them
instantly shift out of reach. A test
of patience: if the net comes too close,
they dart. I keep it almost still, a lazy twitch
now and then. A quick dip and I catch
a single minnow, pull it into the air,
weightless, a flutter in my hand.
I glimpse its silver belly, its round, perfect eye.
In greenish water it was a dart of motion;
now in my cupped palm it seems
made of light, too small to house bones
and heart. I want to look closer, see
beneath its skin, but it loses breath
the longer I hold it. I dip the net
again. The bright thing swims,
regains its element, its grace.

Star Lake

Late evening, the lake turns scarlet,
steel blue, silver. The surface is sharp
on my ankles, a dividing line that moves
as I wade in. A cool finger on knees,
thighs, small of my back.
Then plunge in, kick, and it's warm,
welcoming against my skin.
Water with lustre of molten metal,
colour of flame.

Near the floating dock I stand on tiptoe,
neck-deep, watch the slight waves settle
into calm. Whirligig beetles dart and circle,
polished ovals catching the light. I swim again,
slow strokes, let water move frictionless
over skin. Willing the sunset to stay
poised in this bright instant.
Resisting the return to shore.

Unseen

The deer at first light, who left
her varnished black turds beside
the cabin steps.

The ruffed grouse, camouflaged
on mottled ground, amid grey spruce trunks,
drumming.

The woodpecker, red-crested
driller, leaving cavities
that leak drops
of pungent sap.

The loud marsh-dwellers, hidden
in bent reeds, willows, sedges—
mallards' *ahp-ahp* in the distance,
frog-chorus call and answer
crrik-crrik across the wet expanse
and close by, their shrilling palpable
in the fading light.

Closing the camp

Brown ferns along the roadside, reddened leaves
of strawberry, bunchberry, raspberry
tipped with frost. The morning overcast,
lit only by the aspen leaves still clinging,
pointillistic, to their branches, or scattered,
windblown, caught in dark-green conifers.
We're working down a list: floating dock
pulled onto shore, pails and shovels stowed,
beach chairs hauled indoors. Cupboards emptied,
shelves wiped clean of crumbs, water lines
drained against freeze-up. Mist over the lake
comes and goes, comes and goes. The water's
dull aluminum. Tomorrow the last windows
will be washed, we'll pack our things
and go, waving goodbye, goodnight,
good winter. The flocks of slate-grey juncos
will disperse as each car passes, then return,
tipping their beaks to the ground.

What we don't know about winter

Whether the lake is a field, cross-hatched
with deer and fox tracks.

How much of life goes on,
and how much dies, or sleeps, or flies south.

What burrows under cabin steps.
What shakes hoarfrost from poplar twigs.

Whether the road's been plowed.
If the bench on the hill is buried.

If we'd complain about cold-stiffened fingers.
If our breath would echo.

Whether we'd know the place,
stripped down to grey bark, needles, snow.

If we stood on the shoreline now,
what shapes would pass overhead.

Opening the camp

A chilly May this year,
the last late snow a wisp
in the bush, our feet squelching
through grass by the cabins.
The streamlet along the road
purling lakeward, filling its channel,
a glassy tinkle under the swell
of voices arriving.

We rake debris off the beach,
tarnished leaves from the stream bed.
The men take down a worm-eaten tree,
drag it off to the brush pile.
In the lodge, we clean windows, vacuum
dust and bug wings from the lights.

At dusk, a pair of spruce grouse
emerge in the open, foraging.
We quiet our steps as they feed,
their voices liquid, intimate.

This is spring too

We wake to spatters of white
on the windows, an absurdity of snow
on emerging leaves, grass blades
vivid against wet flakes drifting down.
White-throated sparrows hop,
knee-deep, their striped heads flicking.
We step out the door fluffed up
with sweaters, stumping off toward
whatever's waiting to be done.
Robins run past on yellow feet,
thrushes with plumped-up feathers
peck for whatever they can find.
Tomorrow all this will melt,
but they've got to eat today.

The quiet after

We canoe to the northwest corner,
days after the storm. The lake's
deeper now, lapping the feet
of the birches. On the rocks, a dried slurry
of leaves, waterweeds, crumbled
twigs—last week's high-water mark.
At the creek's mouth, silt lies
ankle-deep, waterlogged. We prod
with a paddle, confirm the rock
is still there underneath. Step out,
sink, slip. Rebalance. Bare feet slurp
in the soft muck. We pick our way
upstream without speaking.
Sheltered here from the lake breeze,
it's hot, still a bit rank-smelling
from the flash flood—those few hours
of pounding rain when the creek
swelled, scraped earth from its banks,
bent and broke the waist-high reeds.
It must have been loud, we say,
barely raising our voices above
the mosquito hum.

Tuck Island

It's just big enough that we can see it
if we head the right direction,
remember where to look;

just high enough that we can pull
canoes up over rock, snag them on bushes
so they don't drift off and leave us;

low enough that, in wet years,
its edges slip into the lake;
barely long enough to have two ends,

one stony, one shrubby, and when the kids
explore the far side, I can almost
hold their hands from here;

enough of it to visit each summer,
share chocolate around the picnic table
that's always been there, weathered, loose-jointed;

room enough for small things: grass, lichen,
dragonflies, and two (one white, one purple)
flowers I've never seen before.

Wildflower chant

water lily white
pond lily yellow

twinflower, bunchberry
yellow avens, yarrow

gooseberry, strawberry
bedstraw, tansy

columbine, wintergreen
harebell, daisy

goat's-beard, cattail
stork's-bill, catchfly

buttercup, coralroot
blue flag, anemone

joe-pye, golden bean
milk vetch, wild pea

starflower, arrowhead
sunflower, fireweed

honeysuckle, meadowsweet
violet, rose

Re-creation

Turning in on the narrow road,
the new smell of woods and water.
First sight of the lake, red dock, birches on the shore.

First dragonflies dip and hover
in the reeds, all eyes
and rapid wings.
Water beetles skim, zigzag,
a scribble on the surface.
The first mosquitoes whine around my ears.

The first touch of water on skin,
my body slipping through currents of warm and cool.
At dusk, the first shivering loon-call.
First setting sun trails red across the lake.

The long light of evening on the beach.
The first night.
The first blue morning.

Notes

How far can we follow

The biblical quotation in "Image in a country church" is from Revelation 5:6 (Revised Standard Version of the Bible, copyright © 1946, 1952, and 1971 National Council of the Churches of Christ in the United States of America. Used by permission. All rights reserved worldwide).

In "Park Valley," the lines in italics are from the hymn "There is a green hill far away" by Cecil Frances Alexander (1818-1895). First published in *Hymns for Little Children* (1848). It is in the public domain.

I used to know the place

In "Bearings," the lines in italics are from posters promoting emigration to Canada in the early 20th century, found online at the Archives Society of Alberta (https://albertaonrecord.ca/land-settlement-and-immigration) and the Canadian Museum of History (https://www.historymuseum.ca/cmc/exhibitions/hist/advertis/ads7-03e.html). When writing this poem, I consulted the *Atlas of Saskatchewan* (edited by Kai-iu Fung, University of Saskatchewan, 1999), particularly the maps entitled "Natural Vegetation," "Land Covers of Southern Saskatchewan," and "Ethnic Bloc Settlements 1850s-1990s."

Blue hills

The epigraph to "Barefoot girls" is from a 2017 TED Talk by Prumsodun Ok, "The magic of Khmer classical dance" (to watch the full talk, visit https://www.ted.com).

In "What they do here," the lines in italics are from a remembered conversation with a cyclo driver in Phnom Penh.

In "Ratana takes me to the market," Mony Ratana was the administrator for Mennonite Central Committee's Phnom Penh office at the time of my visit there in 1994.

Tuol Sleng Genocide Museum is a former secondary school in Phnom Penh that was used as an interrogation and detention centre by the Khmer Rouge.

Vesak Day, a Buddhist holy day that usually falls between late April and early June, celebrates the birth, enlightenment, and death of the Buddha.

Resisting the return to shore

"Minnowing" is for Sally Ito.

"Re-creation" was written for a short film by Kenji Dyck (https://www.youtube.com/watch?v=_ImYmbvL--Y).

Acknowledgements

My current home, Winnipeg, with its rivers and creeks, is on Treaty 1 territory. The places in Saskatchewan where I grew up, and to which I remain connected, lie within Treaty 6 and Treaty 4. The little corner of the Canadian Shield that I have come to know and love lies within Treaty 3. I am grateful for the time I am able to spend in all these places.

My thanks to the editors of the publications in which some of these poems, or earlier versions of them, first appeared: "Chokecherries" in *The Broken City*; "Park Valley" in *Rhubarb*; "Raspberries" in *Curio Poetry*; "Chance" and "Getaway" in *Juniper*; "Retreat" in *Geez*; "Wild strawberries" in *Carleton Arts Review*; "Affirmation" in *Canadian Literature*; "Ratana takes me to the market" and "Tuol Sleng" in *The Antigonish Review*; "In the dome car" in *Prairie Fire* (third-place winner of the 2018 Banff Centre Bliss Carman poetry contest); "Fort Carlton" and "Stopped in the Qu'Appelle Valley" in *The New Quarterly.*

Several poems from the sections "How far can we follow," "I used to know the place," and "Settling into motion" were published as the chapbook *Crossings* in 2012, the culmination of my term as writer-in-residence at St. Margaret's Anglican Church, Winnipeg. My thanks to the Manitoba Arts Council for a grant that helped with the writing of these poems, and to St. Margaret's for providing space and encouragement.

I am grateful for the opportunity to attend the Spring Poetry Colloquium at Sage Hill in 2008 and gain inspiration from birds, wildflowers, and fellow poets.

Thanks especially to instructor Erín Moure for giving me the idea of writing about a creek in the city.

The poems in "Blue hills" resulted from a trip to Cambodia in 1994, while I was working for Mennonite Central Committee in Ottawa. I am grateful for having been given this wonderful opportunity. Many thanks to the MCC staff who arranged my lodging, showed me around Phnom Penh, and let me tag along on a visit to Tram Kak District in Takeo Province.

Many thanks to everyone who read and commented on these poems at various stages: members of the May Day Poetry Project, Jennifer Still, Sally Ito, and especially Angeline Schellenberg. This book is much better because of you.

Thanks to Alice Major for her wise and patient editing, and to everyone at Turnstone Press for bringing this book into the world.

And many thanks and much love to my family.